Random

Modern Standard Arabic

A1

Book 1

lingualism

ISBN: 9798374813869

website: www.lingualism.com

email: contact@lingualism.com

How to Use This Book

Random Modern Standard Arabic is designed to assist beginning learners of the A1 level of Modern Standard Arabic. It contains 250 sentences and phrases, each **numbered for easy reference**. The first are short and gradually get longer.

The sentences are written in **Arabic script** with diacritics. (It's important to remember that diacritics are not spoken before the end of a sentence or clause in Arabic, but they are still written.)

A **phonemic transcription** is provided on the next line for those who need additional assistance in reading Arabic script. Visit www.lingualism.com/pt-msa for our guide to reading phonemic transcription.

An **English translation** is also provided for each sentence.

The book also includes **free audio** recordings, which can be accessed on our website at www.lingualism.com/audio.

The corresponding **track number and time stamp** are provided for each sentence, allowing you to easily match the audio with the text.

The sentences in this book are randomly selected and do not cover all vocabulary for the A1 level, but the repetition of similar structures and vocabulary is intentional to aid in fluency and vocabulary building.

Random Modern Standard Arabic is not just a book to read and listen to, but also a tool to actively practice and improve your language skills. As you work through the sentences, try making variations by changing the persons, places, and objects in each sentence. Practice making negative sentences and try to adapt them to be true for yourself. This book is designed to be interactive and to be used in a way that works best for you. So don't be afraid to experiment and make the sentences your own. The more you practice, the more you'll find your fluency and vocabulary growing.

Sentences that vary depending on gender are given twice, with labels indicating the person and gender.

1M (first-person masculine): how a male speaker would say it.

1F (first-person feminine): how a female speaker would say it.

2M (second-person masculine): how you would say it to a man/boy.

2F (second-person feminine): how you would say it to a woman/girl.

3M (third-person masculine): how you would say it when referring to a man/boy or an inanimate object that is grammatically masculine.

3F (third-person feminine): how you would say it when referring to a woman/girl or an inanimate object that is grammatically feminine.

1

Track 1 - 0:00

أَنا مُتْعَبٌ.

1M *ʔana mut3ab^{un}.*

أَنا مُتْعَبَةٌ.

1F *ʔana mut3aba^{tun}.*

I'm tired.

2

Track 1 - 0:08

لا أَعْلَمُ.

lā ʔa3lam^{u}.

I don't know.

3

Track 1 - 0:11

عَفْوًا.

3afwan.

You're welcome.

4

Track 1 - 0:14

أَنا خائِفٌ.

1M *ʔana xāʔif*^{un}.

أَنا خائِفَةٌ.

1F *ʔana xāʔifa*^{tun}.

I'm afraid.

5

Track 1 - 0:21

لَدَيَّ قِطَّةٌ.

ladayy^{a} *qiṭṭa*^{tun}.

I have a cat.

6

Track 1 - 0:25

أَنا مُمَرِّضٌ.

1M *ʔana mumarriḍ*^{un}.

أَنا مُمَرِّضَةٌ.

1F *ʔana mumarriḍa*^{tun}.

I'm a nurse.

7

Track 1 - 0:32

أَنا أُحِبُّ التُّفّاحَ.

ʔana ʔuħibb^{u} *-ttuffāħ*^{a}*.*

I like apples.

8

Track 1 - 0:37

لِنَأْكُلْ.

li-naʔkul.

Let's eat.

9

Track 1 - 0:40

مَنْ أَنْتَ؟

2M *man ʔant*^{a}*?*

مَنْ أَنْتِ؟

2F *man ʔant*^{i}*?*

Who are you?

10

Track 1 - 0:47

أَنا مُوافِقٌ.

1M *ʔana muwāfiq^{un}.*

أَنا مُوافِقَةٌ.

1F *ʔana muwāfiqa^{tun}.*

I agree.

11

Track 1 - 0:55

مَعَ السَّلامَةِ!

ma3^{a} -ssalāma^{ti}!

Goodbye!

12

Track 1 - 0:59

أُحِبُّ السِّباحَةَ.

ʔuɦibb^{u} -ssibāɦa^{ta}.

I like to swim.

13

Track 1 - 1:03

أَنا مُعَلِّمٌ.

1M *ʔana mu3allim*^{un}.

أَنا مُعَلِّمَةٌ.

1F *ʔana mu3allima*^{tun}.

I'm a teacher.

14

Track 1 - 1:10

أَنا أَشْعَرُ بِالْمَلَلِ.

ʔana ʔaš3ar^{u} *bi-lmalal*^{i}.

I'm bored.

15

Track 1 - 1:15

أَرى كَلْبًا.

ʔarā kalban.

I see a dog.

16

Track 1 - 1:19

كَيْفَ حالُكَ؟

2M *kayf^a ђāluk^a?*

كَيْفَ حالُكِ؟

2F *kayf^a ђāluk^i?*

How are you?

17

Track 1 - 1:26

تَعالَ مَعي.

2M *ta3āl^a ma3ī.*

تَعالي مَعي.

2F *ta3ālī ma3ī.*

Come with me.

18

Track 1 - 1:34

إِنَّها سَعيدَةٌ.

ʔinnahā sa3īda^tun.

She is happy.

19

Track 1 - 1:38

هُوَ طَويلٌ.

huwa ṭawīl^{un}.

He is tall.

20

Track 1 - 1:42

أَنا أَعْتَرِضُ.

ʔana ʔa3tariḍ^{u}.

I disagree.

21

Track 1 - 1:45

أَنا مَريضٌ.

1M *ʔana marīḍ*^{un}.

أَنا مَريضَةٌ.

1F *ʔana marīḍa*^{tun}.

I'm sick.

22

Track 1 - 1:52

هَذا كِتابٌ.

hađā kitāb^{un}.

This is a book.

23

Track 1 - 1:56

نَعَمْ.

na3am.

Yes.

24

Track 1 - 1:59

سَيّارَتي قَديمَةٌ.

sayyāratī qadīma^{tun}.

My car is old.

25

Track 1 - 2:03

اِنْتَظِرْ هُنا.

2M *intaẓir hunā.*

اِنْتَظِري هُنا.

2F *intaẓirī hunā.*

Wait here.

26

Track 1 - 2:11

مَساءَ الخَيْرِ.

masāʔ^{a} -lxayr^{i}.

Good afternoon.

27

Track 1 - 2:15

هُوَ يُحِبُّ البيتْزا.

huwa yuɦibb^u -lbītzā.

He likes pizza.

28

Track 1 - 2:20

أَنا عَطْشانٌ.

1M *ʔana 3aţšān^un.*

أَنا عَطْشانَةٌ.

1F *ʔana 3aţšāna^tun.*

I'm thirsty.

29

Track 1 - 2:27

شُكْرًا لَكَ.

2M *šukran lak^a.*

شُكْرًا لَكِ.

2F *šukran lak^i.*

Thank you.

30

Track 1 - 2:34

مَرْحَبًا!

marђaban!

Hello!

31

Track 1 - 2:37

كَمْ عُمُرُكَ؟

2M *kam 3umuruk^{a}?*

كَمْ عُمُرُكِ؟

2F *kam 3umuruk^{i}?*

How old are you?

32

Track 1 - 2:44

لَدَيَّ تِسْعَةَ عَشَرَ كِتابًا.

ladayy^{a} tis3a^{ta} 3ašar^{a} kitāban.

I have nineteen books.

33

Track 1 - 2:51

لَدَيَّ حَديقَةٌ.

ladayy^{a} ђadīqa^{tun}.

I have a garden.

34

Track 1 - 2:55

لَعِبْتُ كُرَةَ القَدَمِ.

la3ibt^{u} kura^{ta} -lqadam^{i}.

I played soccer.

35

Track 1 - 3:00

أَنا كُنْتُ طالِبًا.

1M *ʔana kunt^{u} ṭāliban.*

أَنا كُنْتُ طالِبَةً.

1F *ʔana kunt^{u} ṭāliba^{tan}.*

I was a student.

36

Track 1 - 3:09

هَلْ هُوَ مُكَلِّفٌ؟

3M *hal huwa mukallif^{un}?*

هَلْ هِيَ مُكَلِّفَةٌ؟

3F *hal hiya mukallifa^{tun}?*

Is it expensive?

37

Track 1 - 3:18

اِسْمي جونْ.

ismī [John].

My name is John.

38

Track 1 - 3:21

لَدَيْنا قِطَّةٌ واحِدَةٌ.

ladaynā qiṭṭa^{tun} *wāɦida*^{tun}.

We have one cat.

39

Track 1 - 3:27

السَّماءُ زَرْقاءُ.

assamāʔ^{u} *zarqāʔ*^{u}.

The sky is blue.

40

Track 1 - 3:31

اِنْتَظِرْ دَقيقَةً.

2M *intaẓir daqīqa*^{tan}.

اِنْتَظِري دَقيقَةً.

2F *intaẓirī daqīqa*^{tan}.

Hold on a minute.

41

Track 1 - 3:40

لَدَيَّ شُرْفَةٌ.

ladayy^a šurfa^tun.

I have a balcony.

42

Track 1 - 3:44

لَدَيَّ مَطْبَخٌ.

ladayy^a maṭbax^un.

I have a kitchen.

43

Track 1 - 3:48

أَنا أَعيشُ في لَنْدَنْ.

ʔana ʔaʒīš^u fī landan.

I live in London.

44

Track 1 - 3:53

أُريدُ مُثَلَّجاتٍ.

ʔurīd^u mutallajāt^in.

I want ice cream.

45

Track 1 - 3:58

لَيْسَ لَدَيْنا أَيُّ نُقودٍ.

lays^a ladaynā ʔayy^u nuqūd^in.

We don't have any money.

46

Track 1 - 4:04

كانَ هاتِفي جَديدًا.

kān^a hātifī jadīdan.

My phone was new.

47

Track 1 - 4:09

هِيَ صَديقَتي.

hiya ṣadīqatī.

She is my friend.

48

Track 1 - 4:13

هَذا قَلَمُ رَصاصٍ.

hađā qalam^u raṣāṣ^in.

This is a pencil.

49

Track 1 - 4:19

ما اسْمُكَ؟

2M *mā -smuk^{a}?*

ما اسْمُكِ؟

2F *mā -smuk^{i}?*

What is your name?

50

Track 1 - 4:25

إِنَّها تُمْطِرُ الآنَ.

innahā tumṭir^{u} -lʔān^{a}.

It is raining now.

51

Track 2 - 0:00

ما وَزْنُكَ؟

2M *mā waznuk^{a}?*

ما وَزْنُكِ؟

2F *mā waznuk^{i}?*

What is your weight?

52

Track 2 - 0:07

لَدَيَّ تِلِفِزْيونٌ.

ladayy^{a} *tilifizyūn*^{un}*.*

I have a television.

53

Track 2 - 0:12

الجَوُّ مُشْمِسٌ اليَوْمَ.

aljaww^{u} *mušmis*^{uni} *-lyawm*^{a}*.*

It is sunny today.

54

Track 2 - 0:18

ذَهَبْتُ إِلى صالَةِ الألعابِ الرّياضِيَّةِ.

đahabt^{u} *ʔilā ṣāla*^{ti} *-lʔl3āb*^{i} *-rryāḍiyya*^{ti}*.*

I went to the gym.

55

Track 2 - 0:26

أَتَناوَلُ غَذائي عِنْدَ الظَّهيرَةِ.

ʔatanāwal^{u} *ɣađāʔī 3ind*^{a} *-ẓẓahīra*^{ti}*.*

I have lunch at noon.

56

Track 2 - 0:32

سَأُنَظِّفُ غُرْفَتي.

sa-ʔunaz̧z̧if^{u} ɣurfatī.

I will clean my room.

57

Track 2 - 0:37

عِنْدي أَصْدِقاءٌ كَثيرونَ.

3indī ʔaşdiqāʔ^{un} kaṯīrūn^{a}.

I have many friends.

58

Track 2 - 0:43

أَنا لا أَشْرَبُ القَهْوَةَ.

ʔana lā ʔašrab^{u} -lqahwa^{ta}.

I don't drink coffee.

59

Track 2 - 0:48

أَشْعُرُ بِصُداعٍ.

ʔaš3ur^{u} bi-şudā3^{in}.

I have a headache.

60

Track 2 - 0:53

ذَهَبْتُ إِلى المَتْجَرِ.

đahabt^u ʔilā -lmatjar^i.

I went to the store.

61

Track 2 - 0:58

أَنا أَتَعَلَّمُ العَرَبِيَّةَ.

ʔana ʔata3allam^u -l3arabiyya^ta.

I'm learning Arabic.

62

Track 2 - 1:03

ما هُوَ تَخَصُّصُكَ؟

2M *mā huwa taxaşşuşuk^a?*

ما هُوَ تَخَصُّصُكِ؟

2F *mā huwa taxaşşuşuk^i?*

What is your major?

63

Track 2 - 1:13

هَلْ يُمْكِنُكَ الجَرْيُ بِسُرْعَةٍ؟

2M *hal yumkinuk*^{a} *-ljary*^{u} *bi-sur3a*^{tin}*?*

هَلْ يُمْكِنُكِ الجَرْيُ بِسُرْعَةٍ؟

2F *hal yumkinuk*^{i} *-ljary*^{u} *bi-sur3a*^{tin}*?*

Can you run fast?

64

Track 2 - 1:25

أَنا أعيشُ في مَنْزِلٍ.

ʔana ʔ3īš^{u} *fī manzil*^{in}*.*

I live in a house.

65

Track 2 - 1:30

لا أَفْهَمُ.

lā ʔafham^{u}*.*

I don't understand.

66

Track 2 - 1:33

هَذِهِ فِكْرَةٌ سَيِّئَةٌ.

hađih^{i} *fikra*^{tun} *sayyiʔa*^{tun}*.*

That is a bad idea.

67

Track 2 - 1:39

هَلْ أَنْتَ طَويلٌ أَمْ قَصيرٌ؟

2M *hal ʔant*^{a} *ţawīl*^{un} *ʔam qaşīr*^{un}*?*

هَلْ أَنْتِ طَويلَةٌ أَمْ قَصيرَةٌ؟

2F *hal ʔant*^{i} *ţawīla*^{tun} *ʔam qaşīra*^{tun}*?*

Are you tall or short?

68

Track 2 - 1:51

سَأَذْهَبُ لِلتَّسَوُّقِ.

sa-ʔađhab^{u} *li-ttasawwuq*^{i}*.*

I will go shopping.

69

Track 2 - 1:56

سَأَقْرَأُ كِتابًا.

sa-ʔaqraʔ^{u} *kitāban.*

I will read a book.

70

Track 2 - 2:01

لَيْسَ لَدَيَّ سَيّارَةٌ.

lays^{a} *ladayy*^{a} *sayyāra*^{tun}*.*

I don't have a car.

71

Track 2 - 2:06

لَدَيَّ غُرْفَةُ طَعامٍ.

ladayy^{a} ɣurfa^{tu} ţa3ām^{in}.

I have a dining room.

72

Track 2 - 2:12

ذَلِكَ مُثيرٌ لِلاهْتِمامِ.

đalik^{a} muŧīr^{un} li-lihtimām^{i}.

That is interesting.

73

Track 2 - 2:18

أَنا لا أَتَعَلَّمُ الإِنْجِليزِيَّةَ.

ʔana lā ʔata3allam^{u} -lʔinjilīziyya^{ta}.

I'm not learning English.

74

Track 2 - 2:24

لَدَيَّ ثَلاثَةُ كُتُبٍ.

ladayy^{a} ŧalāŧa^{tu} kutub^{in}.

I have three books.

75

Track 2 - 2:29

عُمْري واحِدَةٌ وَعِشْرونَ سَنَةً.

3umrī wāɧida^{tun} wa-3išrūn^{a} sana^{tan}.

I'm twenty-one years old.

76

Track 2 - 2:36

أَنا أَعْمَلُ في أَحَدِ المَكاتِبِ.

ʔana ʔa3mal^{u} fī ʔaɧad^{i} -lmakātib^{i}.

I work in an office.

77

Track 2 - 2:43

هَلْ تُحِبُّ الشّوكولا؟

2M *hal tuɧibb^{u} -ššūkūlā?*

هَلْ تُحِبّينَ الشّوكولا؟

2F *hal tuɧibbīn^{a} -ššūkūlā?*

Do you like chocolate?

78

Track 2 - 2:53

هَلْ تُحِبُّ الرِّياضَةَ؟

2M *hal tuɦibb^{u} -rriyāḍa^{ta}?*

هَلْ تُحِبّينَ الرِّياضَةَ؟

2F *hal tuɦibbīn^{a} -rriyāḍa^{ta}?*

Do you like sports?

79

Track 2 - 3:02

ماذا يَفْعَلُ الآنَ؟

māđā yaf3al^{u} -lʔān^{a}?

What is he doing now?

80

Track 2 - 3:07

أَيْنَ أَنْتَ الآنَ؟

2M *ʔayn^{a} ʔant^{a} -lʔān^{a}?*

أَيْنَ أَنْتِ الآنَ؟

2F *ʔayn^{a} ʔant^{i} -lʔān^{a}?*

Where are you now?

81

Track 2 - 3:16

مَرْحَبًا! كَيْفَ حالُكَ؟

2M *marɧaban! kayfa ɧālukа?*

مَرْحَبًا! كَيْفَ حالُكِ؟

2F *marɧaban! kayfa ɧāluki?*

Hello! How are you?

82

Track 2 - 3:30

هَلْ تَتَحَدَّثُ الإنْجِليزِيَّةَ؟

2M *hal tataɧaddaŧu -lʔinjilīziyyata?*

هَلْ تَتَحَدَّثينَ الإنْجِليزِيَّةَ؟

2F *hal tataɧaddaŧīna -lʔinjilīziyyata?*

Do you speak English?

83

Track 2 - 3:42

هَلْ تَفْهَمُ؟

2M *hal tafhamu?*

هَلْ تَفْهَمينَ؟

2F *hal tafhamīna?*

Do you understand?

84

Track 2 - 3:49

هَلْ تَمْلِكُ سَيّارَةً؟

2M *hal tamlik^{u} sayyāra^{tan}?*

هَلْ تَمْلِكِينَ سَيّارَةً؟

2F *hal tamlikīn^{a} sayyāra^{tan}?*

Do you have a car?

85

Track 2 - 3:58

الرَّجُلُ العَجوزُ حَكيمٌ.

arrajul^{u} -l3ajūz^{u} ɧakīm^{un}.

The old man is wise.

86

Track 2 - 4:04

أُحِبُّ مُشاهَدَةَ التِّلْفازِ.

ʔuɧibb^{u} mušāhada^{ta} -ttilfāz^{i}.

I like to watch TV.

87

Track 2 - 4:10

هُوَ يَأْكُلُ الغَداءَ عِنْدَ الظُّهْرِ.

huwa yaʔkul^{u} -lɣadāʔ^{a} 3ind^{a} -ẓẓuhr^{i}.

He eats lunch at noon.

88

Track 2 - 4:16

لَدَيَّ عَشَرَةُ أَصابِعَ.

ladayy^a 3ašara^tu ʔaṣābi3^a.

I have ten fingers.

89

Track 2 - 4:22

كَمْ وَزْنُهُ؟

3M *kam waznuh^u?*

كَمْ وَزْنُها؟

3F *kam waznuhā?*

How heavy is it?

90

Track 2 - 4:28

لَدَيَّ حَمّامٌ.

ladayy^a ɧammām^un.

I have a bathroom.

91

Track 2 - 4:32

لِنَأْخُذَ اسْتِراحَةً.

li-naʔxuđ^a -stirāɧa^tan.

Let's take a break.

92

Track 2 - 4:37

هَلْ تَذْهَبُ إِلى صالَةِ الأَلْعابِ الرِّياضِيَّةِ؟

2M *hal tađhab*^{u} *ʔilā ṣāla*^{ti} *-lʔal3āb*^{i} *-rriyāḍiyya*^{ti}*?*

هَلْ تَذْهَبينَ إِلى صالَةِ الأَلْعابِ الرِّياضِيَّةِ؟

2F *hal tađhabīn*^{a} *ʔilā ṣāla*^{ti} *-lʔal3āb*^{i} *-rriyāḍiyya*^{ti}*?*

Do you go to the gym?

93

Track 2 - 4:53

يَبْلُغُ مِنَ العُمْرِ سَبْعَ عَشْرَةَ سَنَةً.

yabluɣ^{u} *min*^{a} *-l3umr*^{i} *sab3*^{a} *3ašra*^{ta} *sana*^{tan}*.*

He is seventeen years old.

94

Track 2 - 5:01

سَوْفَ أَذْهَبُ إِلى صالَةِ الأَلْعابِ الرِّياضِيَّةِ.

sawf^{a} *ʔađhab*^{u} *ʔilā ṣāla*^{ti} *-lʔal3āb*^{i} *-rriyāḍiyya*^{ti}*.*

I will go to the gym.

95

Track 2 - 5:09

هَذا الكِتابُ ثَقيلٌ.

hađā -lkitāb^{u} *ŧaqīl*^{un}*.*

This book is heavy.

96

Track 2 - 5:14

سَوْفَ أُشاهِدُ فيلْمًا.

sawf^{a} ʔušāhid^{u} fīlman.

I will watch a movie.

97

Track 2 - 5:20

هَلْ لَدَيْكَ أَيُّ حَيَواناتٍ أَليفَةٍ؟

2M *hal ladayk^{a} ʔayy^{u} ɧayawānāt^{in} ʔalīfa^{tin}?*

هَلْ لَدَيْكِ أَيُّ حَيَواناتٍ أَليفَةٍ؟

2F *hal ladayk^{i} ʔayy^{u} ɧayawānāt^{in} ʔalīfa^{tin}?*

Do you have any pets?

98

Track 2 - 5:34

إِلى أَيْنَ تَذْهَبُ؟

2M *ʔilā ʔayn^{a} tađhab^{u}?*

إِلى أَيْنَ تَذْهَبينَ؟

2F *ʔilā ʔayn^{a} tađhabīn^{a}?*

Where are you going?

99

Track 2 - 5:43

ذَهَبْتُ إِلى الحَديقَةِ.

đahabt^u ʔilā -lħadīqa^ti.

I went to the park.

100

Track 2 - 5:48

شاهَدْتُ فيلْمًا.

šāhadt^u fīlman.

I watched a movie.

101

Track 3 - 0:00

لَنْ أَذْهَبَ إِلى المَدْرَسَةِ غَدًا.

lan ʔađhab^a ʔilā -lmadrasa^ti ɣadan.

I'm not going to school tomorrow.

102

Track 3 - 0:06

إِنَّهُ لا يُحِبُّ المُثَلَّجاتِ.

ʔinnah^u lā yuħibb^u -lmuŧallajāt^i.

He doesn't like ice cream.

103

Track 3 - 0:13

لَدَيَّ كَلْبٌ وَقِطَّةٌ.

ladayy^{a} *kalb*^{un} *wa-qiţţa*^{tun}.

I have a dog and a cat.

104

Track 3 - 0:18

أَخي طَبيبٌ.

ʔaxī ţabīb^{un}.

My brother is a doctor.

105

Track 3 - 0:22

أَنا ذاهِبٌ إِلى الحَديقَةِ.

1M *ʔana đāhib*^{un} *ʔilā -lɦadīqa*^{ti}.

أَنا ذاهِبَةٌ إِلى الحَديقَةِ.

1F *ʔana đāhiba*^{tun} *ʔilā -lɦadīqa*^{ti}.

I'm going to the park.

106

Track 3 - 0:34

أَذْهَبُ إِلى المَدْرَسَةِ بِالْحافِلَةِ.

ʔađhab^{u} *ʔilā -lmadrasa*^{ti} *bi-lɦāfila*^{ti}.

I go to school by bus.

107

Track 3 - 0:40

ما هِيَ وَظيفَتُكَ؟

2M *mā hiya waz̧īfatuk*^{a}*?*

ما هِيَ وَظيفَتُكِ؟

2F *mā hiya waz̧īfatuk*^{i}*?*

What is your job?

108

Track 3 - 0:49

هِيَ لَنْ تَقْرَأَ كِتابًا.

hiya lan taqraʔ^{a} *kitāban.*

She will not read a book.

109

Track 3 - 0:54

إِنَّهُ يُعِدُّ العَشاءَ الآنَ.

ʔinnah^{u} *yu3idd*^{u} *-l3ašāʔ*^{a} *-lʔān*^{a}*.*

He is making dinner now.

110

Track 3 - 1:00

إِنَّها تُمْطِرُ في الخارِجِ.

ʔinnahā tumţir^{u} *fī -lxārij*^{i}*.*

It is raining outside.

111

Track 3 - 1:06

سَأَذْهَبُ إِلى الفِراشِ مُبَكِّرًا.

sa-ʔađhab^{u} *ʔilā -lfirāš*^{i} *mubakkiran.*

I will go to bed early.

112

Track 3 - 1:13

لَدَيَّ أُخْتٌ واحِدَةٌ صَغيرَةٌ.

ladayy^{a} *ʔuxt*^{un} *wāħida*^{tun} *ṣaɣīra*^{tun}.

I have one younger sister.

113

Track 3 - 1:20

لَدَيَّ الكَثيرُ مِنَ المالِ.

ladayy^{a} *-lkaŧīr*^{u} *min*^{a} *-lmāl*^{i}.

I have a lot of money.

114

Track 3 - 1:26

عَمِلْتُ في مَكْتَبٍ.

3amilt^{u} *fī maktab*^{in}.

I worked in an office.

115

Track 3 - 1:30

هِيَ لا تَعْزِفُ الموسيقى.

hiya lā ta3zif^{u} -lmūsīqā.

She is not playing music.

116

Track 3 - 1:36

أَنا لا أَتَناوَلُ الفُطورَ.

ʔana lā ʔatanāwal^{u} -lfuṭūr^{a}.

I don't eat breakfast.

117

Track 3 - 1:42

كانَ الكِتابُ عَلى الطّاوِلَةِ.

kān^{a} -lkitāb^{u} 3alā -ṭṭāwila^{ti}.

The book was on the table.

118

Track 3 - 1:47

هَلْ لَدَيْكَ أَيُّ أَصْدِقاءٍ؟

2M *hal ladayk^{a} ʔayy^{u} ʔaṣdiqāʔ^{in}?*

هَلْ لَدَيْكِ أَيُّ أَصْدِقاءٍ؟

2F *hal ladayk^{i} ʔayy^{u} ʔaṣdiqāʔ^{in}?*

Do you have any friends?

119

Track 3 - 1:59

أَنا سَعيدٌ لِمُقابَلَتِكَ.

2M *ʔana sa3īd*^{un} *li-muqābalatik*^{a}.

أَنا سَعيدَةٌ لِمُقابَلَتِكِ.

2F *ʔana sa3īda*^{tun} *li-muqābalatik*^{i}.

I'm glad to meet you.

120

Track 3 - 2:11

لَّوْني المُفَضَّلُ هُوَ الأَزْرَقُ.

llawnī -lmufaḍḍal^{u} *huwa -lʔazraq*^{u}.

My favorite color is blue.

121

Track 3 - 2:18

هَلْ ذَهَبَ إِلى المَتْجَرِ؟

hal đahab^{a} *ʔilā -lmatjar*^{i}?

Did he go to the store?

122

Track 3 - 2:23

هَلْ يُمْكِنُكَ مُساعَدَتي في هَذا؟

2M *hal yumkinuk^{a} musā3adatī fī hađā?*

هَلْ يُمْكِنُكِ مُساعَدَتي في هَذا؟

2F *hal yumkinuk^{i} musā3adatī fī hađā?*

Can you help me with this?

123

Track 3 - 2:37

كانَ لَدَيَّ الكَثيرُ مِنَ الواجِباتِ المَدْرَسِيَّةِ.

kān^{a} ladayy^{a} -lkaŧīr^{u} min^{a} -lwājibāt^{i} -lmadrasiyya^{ti}.

I had a lot of homework.

124

Track 3 - 2:46

أَعيشُ في بَلْدَةٍ صَغيرَةٍ.

ʔa3īš^{u} fī balda^{tin} şaɣīra^{tin}.

I live in a small town.

125

Track 3 - 2:52

القِطُّ الأَسْوَدُ كَبيرٌ في السِّنِّ.

alqiţţ^{u} -lʔaswad^{u} kabīr^{un} fī -ssinn^{i}.

The black cat is old.

126

Track 3 - 2:59

سَأُمْضي وَقْتًا مُمْتِعًا.

sa-ʔumḍī waqtan mumti3an.

I will have a good time.

127

Track 3 - 3:04

أُحِبُّ لَعِبَ التِّنِسِ.

ʔuḫibbᵘ la3ibᵃ -ttinisⁱ.

I like to play tennis.

128

Track 3 - 3:09

سَوْفَ أُشاهِدُ التِّلْفازَ.

sawfᵃ ʔušāhidᵘ -ttilfāzᵃ.

I will watch television.

129

Track 3 - 3:15

نَعَمْ، أَنا أُحِبُّ الموسيقى.

na3am, ʔana ʔuḫibbᵘ -lmūsīqā.

Yes, I love music.

130

Track 3 - 3:22

هَلْ يُحِبُّ المُثَلَّجاتِ؟

hal yuħibbᵘ -lmuŧallajātⁱ?

Does he like ice cream?

131

Track 3 - 3:28

أَنا لَسْتُ عَلى ما يُرامُ.

ʔana lastᵘ 3alā mā yurāmᵘ.

I'm not feeling well.

132

Track 3 - 3:33

لَمْ أُقابِلْ أَيَّ شَخْصٍ جَديدٍ.

lam ʔuqābil ʔayyᵃ šaxṣⁱⁿ jadīdⁱⁿ.

I did not meet anyone new.

133

Track 3 - 3:40

هَلْ لَدَيْكَ أَيُّ أَشِقّاءٍ؟

2M *hal ladaykᵃ ʔayyᵘ ʔašiqqāʔⁱⁿ?*

هَلْ لَدَيْكِ أَيُّ أَشِقّاءٍ؟

2F *hal ladaykⁱ ʔayyᵘ ʔašiqqāʔⁱⁿ?*

Do you have any siblings?

134

Track 3 - 3:51

ماذا تَعْمَلُ؟

2M *mādā ta3mal*^{u}*?*

ماذا تَعْمَلينَ؟

2F *mādā ta3malīn*^{a}*?*

What do you do for work?

135

Track 3 - 4:00

أَنا أُعاني مِنَ الحَساسِيَّةِ مِنَ الفولِ السّودانِيِّ.

ʔana ʔu3ānī min^{a} *-lħasāsiyya*^{ti} *min*^{a} *-lfūl*^{i} *-ssūdāniyy*^{i}*.*

I'm allergic to peanuts.

136

Track 3 - 4:09

كَمْ مَرَّةً تَتَمَرَّنُ؟

2M *kam marra*^{tan} *tatamarran*^{u}*?*

كَمْ مَرَّةً تَتَمَرَّنينَ؟

2F *kam marra*^{tan} *tatamarranīn*^{a}*?*

How often do you exercise?

137

Track 3 - 4:20

الطَّقْسُ سَيِّءٌ اليَوْمَ.

aṭṭaqs^{u} *sayyiʔ*^{uni} *-lyawm*^{a}.

The weather is bad today.

138

Track 3 - 4:25

زُرْتُ جَدَّتي.

zurt^{u} *jaddatī.*

I visited my grandmother.

139

Track 3 - 4:30

أنا أَذْهَبُ إِلى المَدْرَسَةِ كُلَّ يَوْمٍ.

ʔana ʔađhab^{u} *ʔilā -lmadrasa*^{ti} *kull*^{a} *yawm*^{in}.

I go to school every day.

140

Track 3 - 4:37

لَدَيَّ غَسّالَةٌ.

ladayy^{a} *ɣassāla*^{tun}.

I have a washing machine.

141

Track 3 - 4:42

أُحِبُّ سَماعَ الموسيقى.

ʔuɦibb^{u} samā3^{a} -lmūsīqā.

I like to listen to music.

142

Track 3 - 4:47

أُمّي تَبْلُغُ مِنَ العُمْرِ خَمْسينَ عامًا.

ʔummī tabluɣ^{u} min^{a} -l3umr^{i} xamsīn^{a} 3āman.

My mother is fifty years old.

143

Track 3 - 4:55

سَأَذْهَبُ إِلى المَتْجَرِ.

sa-ʔađhab^{u} ʔilā -lmatjar^{i}.

I'm going to go to the store.

144

Track 3 - 5:00

إِنَّها تَتَحَدَّثُ عَلى الهاتِفِ.

ʔinnahā tataɦaddaŧ^{u} 3alā -lhātif^{i}.

She talks on the phone.

145

Track 3 - 5:07

أَسْعَدَتْني رُؤْيَتُكَ.

2M *ʔas3adatnī ruʔyatuk[a].*

أَسْعَدَتْني رُؤْيَتُكِ.

2F *ʔas3adatnī ruʔyatuk[i].*

I was happy to see you.

146

Track 3 - 5:17

كانَتْ لَدَيَّ قِطَّةٌ رَمادِيَّةٌ.

kānat ladayy[a] qiṭṭa[tun] ramādiyya[tun].

I used to have a gray cat.

147

Track 3 - 5:24

سَأُذاكِرُ لِامْتِحاناتي.

sa-ʔuđākir[u] li-mtiḫānātī.

I will study for my exams.

148

Track 3 - 5:30

ذاكَرْتُ لِامْتِحاناتي.

đākart[u] li-mtiḫānātī.

I studied for my exams.

149

Track 3 - 5:35

شُكْرًا لَكَ عَلى مُساعَدَتِكَ.

2M *šukran lak^a 3alā musā3adatik^a.*

شُكْرًا لَكِ عَلى مُساعَدَتِكِ.

2F *šukran lak^i 3alā musā3adatik^i.*

Thank you for your help.

150

Track 3 - 5:48

لَمْ أَرَ أُخْتي.

lam ʔara ʔuxtī.

I did not see my sister.

151

Track 4 - 0:00

ما هِيَ رياضَتُكَ المُفَضَّلَةُ؟

2M *mā hiya ryāḍatuk^a -lmufaḍḍala^tu?*

ما هِيَ رياضَتُكِ المُفَضَّلَةُ؟

2F *mā hiya ryāḍatuk^i -lmufaḍḍala^tu?*

What is your favorite sport?

152

Track 4 - 0:12

هِيَ لا تُذاكِرُ الآنَ.

hiya lā tuđākir^{u} *-lʔān*^{a}*.*

She is not studying right now.

153

Track 4 - 0:17

هَلْ يُمْكِنُني الدَّفْعُ بِواسِطَةِ بِطاقَةِ الِائْتِمانِ؟

hal yumkinunī -ddaf3^{u} *bi-wāsiṭa*^{ti} *biṭāqa*^{ti} *-liʔtimān*^{i}*?*

Can I pay with a credit card?

154

Track 4 - 0:27

لَنْ يَعْمَلوا.

lan ya3malū.

They are not going to work.

155

Track 4 - 0:31

مَدْرَسَتي بِالْقُرْبِ مِنْ مَنْزِلي.

madrasatī bi-lqurb^{i} *min manzilī.*

My school is near my house.

156

Track 4 - 0:37

أَنْتَ لا تَسْتَمِعُ إِلى الرّادْيو.

2M *ʔant^a lā tastami3^u ʔilā -rrādyū.*

أَنْتِ لا تَسْتَمِعينَ إِلى الرّادْيو.

2F *ʔant^i lā tastami3īn^a ʔilā -rrādyū.*

You are not listening to the radio.

157

Track 4 - 0:50

مَنْ سَيَأْتي إِلى الحَفْلَةِ؟

man sa-yaʔtī ʔilā -lḫafla^ti?

Who will come to the party?

158

Track 4 - 0:55

أَنا لَنْ أَذْهَبَ إِلى المَتْجَرِ.

ʔana lan ʔađhab^a ʔilā -lmatjar^i.

I'm not going to go to the store.

159

Track 4 - 1:01

أَذْهَبُ إِلى المَدْرَسَةِ السّاعَةَ الثّامِنَةَ صَباحًا.

ʔađhab^u ʔilā -lmadrasa^ti -ssā3a^ta -ŧŧāmina^ta şabāḫan.

I go to school at eight o'clock.

160

Track 4 - 1:11

نَحْنُ لا نَحْظى بِوَقْتٍ مُمْتِعٍ.

naħnu lā naħẓā bi-waqt^{in} mumti3^{in}.

We are not having a good time.

161

Track 4 - 1:17

لَمْ آكُلْ في مَطْعَمٍ.

lam ʔākul fī maṭ3am^{in}.

I did not eat at a restaurant.

162

Track 4 - 1:22

ماذا تَفْعَلُ الآنَ؟

2M *māđā taf3al^{u} -lʔān^{a}?*

ماذا تَفْعَلينَ الآنَ؟

2F *māđā taf3alīn^{a} -lʔān^{a}?*

What are you doing right now?

163

Track 4 - 1:33

تُغادِرُ الحافِلَةُ السّاعَةَ السّابِعَةَ صَباحًا.

tuɣādir^{u} -lħāfila^{tu} -ssā3a^{ta} -ssābi3a^{ta} ṣabāħan.

The bus leaves at seven o'clock.

164

Track 4 - 1:42

لِماذا لا يُحِبُّ المُثَلَّجاتِ؟

limāđā lā yuɧibb^{u} -lmuŧallajāt^{i}?

Why doesn't he like ice cream?

165

Track 4 - 1:49

سَوْفَ آكُلُ في مَطْعَمٍ.

sawf^{a} ʔākul^{u} fī maʈ3am^{in}.

I will eat at a restaurant.

166

Track 4 - 1:55

هَلْ يُمْكِنُكَ مُساعَدَتي في حَمْلِ هَذِهِ الحَقيبَةِ؟

2M *hal yumkinuk^{a} musā3adatī fī ɧaml^{i} hađih^{i} -lɧaqība^{ti}?*

هَلْ يُمْكِنُكِ مُساعَدَتي في حَمْلِ هَذِهِ الحَقيبَةِ؟

2F *hal yumkinuk^{i} musā3adatī fī ɧaml^{i} hađih^{i} -lɧaqība^{ti}?*

Can you help me carry this bag?

167

Track 4 - 2:13

ما هُوَ عُنْوانُ بَريدِكَ الإِلِكْتُرونيِّ؟

2M *mā huwa 3unwān^{u} barīdik^{a} -lʔilikturūnyy^{i}?*

ما هُوَ عُنْوانُ بَريدِكِ الإِلِكْتُرونيِّ؟

2F *mā huwa 3unwān^{u} barīdik^{i} -lʔilikturūnyy^{i}?*

What is your email address?

168

Track 4 - 2:28

أَقْرَأُ الكُتُبَ في وَقْتِ فَراغي.

ʔaqraʔ^{u} -lkutub^{a} fī waqt^{i} farāɣī.

I read books in my free time.

169

Track 4 - 2:35

أَنا لا أُشاهِدُ التِّلْفازَ.

ʔana lā ʔušāhid^{u} -ttilfāz^{a}.

I'm not watching television.

170

Track 4 - 2:40

هِيَ سَوْفَ تَلْعَبُ كُرَةَ القَدَمِ اليَوْمَ.

hiya sawf^{a} tal3ab^{u} kura^{ta} -lqadam^{i} -lyawm^{a}.

She is going to play soccer today.

171

Track 4 - 2:48

سَوْفَ أَتَعَلَّمُ لُغَةً جَديدَةً.

sawf^{a} ʔata3allam^{u} luɣa^{tan} jadīda^{tan}.

I will learn a new language.

172

Track 4 - 2:54

نَحْنُ لا نُمارِسُ الرِّياضَةَ.

naђnu lā numāris^{u} -rriyāḍa^{ta}.

We don't play sports.

173

Track 4 - 3:00

الكَعْكَةُ اللَّذيذَةُ حُلْوَةٌ.

alka3ka^{tu} -llađīđa^{tu} ђulwa^{tun}.

The delicious cake is sweet.

174

Track 4 - 3:06

هَلْ أَنْتَ رياضِيُّ القَوامِ أَمْ نَحيفٌ؟

2M *hal ʔant^{a} ryāḍiyy^{u} -lqawām^{i} ʔam naђīf^{un}?*

هَلْ أَنْتِ رياضِيَّةُ القَوامِ أَمْ نَحيفَةٌ؟

2F *hal ʔant^{i} ryāḍiyya^{tu} -lqawām^{i} ʔam naђīfa^{tun}?*

Are you athletic or skinny?

175

Track 4 - 3:21

هَلْ يُمْكِنُكَ تَكْرارُ ذَلِكَ مِنْ فَضْلِكَ؟

2M *hal yumkinuk^{a} takrār^{u} đalik^{a} min faḑlik^{a}?*

هَلْ يُمْكِنُكِ تَكْرارُ ذَلِكَ مِنْ فَضْلِكِ؟

2F *hal yumkinuk^{i} takrār^{u} đalik^{a} min faḑlik^{i}?*

Can you repeat that, please?

176

Track 4 - 3:37

كَمْ مِنَ المالِ لَدَيْكَ؟

2M *kam min^{a} -lmāl^{i} ladayk^{a}?*

كَمْ مِنَ المالِ لَدَيْكِ؟

2F *kam min^{a} -lmāl^{i} ladayk^{i}?*

How much money do you have?

177

Track 4 - 3:47

هَلْ يُمْكِنُكَ أَنْ تُرِيَنِي عَلَى الخَرِيطَةِ؟

2M *hal yumkinuk^{a} ʔan turyanī 3alā -lxarīţa^{ti}?*

هَلْ يُمْكِنُكِ أَنْ تُرِينِيَ عَلَى الخَرِيطَةِ؟

2F *hal yumkinuk^{i} ʔan turīnī 3alā -lxarīţa^{ti}?*

Can you show me on the map?

178

Track 4 - 4:01

ما هِيَ هِوايَتُكَ المُفَضَّلَةُ؟

2M *mā hiya hiwāyatuk^{a} -lmufaḍḍala^{tu}?*

ما هِيَ هِوايَتُكِ المُفَضَّلَةُ؟

2F *mā hiya hiwāyatuk^{i} -lmufaḍḍala^{tu}?*

What is your favorite hobby?

179

Track 4 - 4:13

كَمْ عَدَدُ الحِصَصِ لَدَيْكَ؟

2M *kam 3adad^{u} -lḫiṣaṣ^{i} ladayk^{a}?*

كَمْ عَدَدُ الحِصَصِ لَدَيْكِ؟

2F *kam 3adad^{u} -lḫiṣaṣ^{i} ladayk^{i}?*

How many classes do you have?

180

Track 4 - 4:25

أَحْتاجُ لِشِراءِ الحَليبِ وَالْخُبْزِ.

ʔaḫtāj^{u} li-širāʔ^{i} -lḫalīb^{i} wa-lxubz^{i}.

I need to buy milk and bread.

181

Track 4 - 4:32

أَنا آسِفٌ، لا أَفْهَمُ.

1M *ʔana ʔāsif^{un}, lā ʔafham^{u}.*

أَنا آسِفَةٌ، لا أَفْهَمُ.

1F *ʔana ʔāsifa^{tun}, lā ʔafham^{u}.*

I'm sorry, I don't understand.

182

Track 4 - 4:44

الموسيقى الصّاخِبَةُ مُزْعِجَةٌ.

almūsīqā -ṣṣāxiba^{tu} muz3ija^{tun}.

The loud music is annoying.

183

Track 4 - 4:51

أَنا أَتَحَدَّثُ الإِنْجِليزِيَّةَ وَالْعَرَبِيَّةَ.

ʔana ʔataħaddaŧ^{u} -lʔinjilīziyya^{ta} wa-l3arabiyya^{ta}.

I speak English and Arabic.

184

Track 4 - 4:59

ما هُوَ طَعامُكَ المُفَضَّلُ؟

2M *mā huwa ṭa3āmuk^{a} -lmufaḍḍal^{u}?*

ما هُوَ طَعامُكِ المُفَضَّلُ؟

2F *mā huwa ṭa3āmuk^{i} -lmufaḍḍal^{u}?*

What is your favorite food?

185

Track 4 - 5:10

إِنَّهُ يَذْهَبُ إِلى صالَةِ الأَلْعابِ الرّياضِيَّةِ يَوْمِيًّا.

ʔinnah^{u} yađhab^{u} ʔilā ṣāla^{ti} -lʔal3āb^{i} -rryāḍiyya^{ti} yawmiyyan.

He goes to the gym every day.

186

Track 4 - 5:21

كُنْتُ بِحاجَةٍ للذَّهابِ إِلى الحَمّامِ.

kunt^{u} bi-ḥāja^{tin} li-đđahāb^{i} ʔilā -lḥammām^{i}.

I needed to go to the bathroom.

187

Track 4 - 5:28

يُمْكِنُني السِّباحَةُ وَرُكوبُ الدَّرّاجَةِ.

yumkinunī -ssibāḥa^{tu} wa-rukūb^{u} -ddarrāja^{ti}.

I can swim and ride a bike.

188

Track 4 - 5:37

هَلْ لَدَيْكَ أَيُّ أَهْدافٍ لِللِّياقَةِ؟

2M *hal ladayk^a ʔayy^u ʔahdāf^in li-llliyāqa^ti?*

هَلْ لَدَيْكِ أَيُّ أَهْدافٍ لِللِّياقَةِ؟

2F *hal ladayk^i ʔayy^u ʔahdāf^in li-llliyāqa^ti?*

Do you have any fitness goals?

189

Track 4 - 5:50

هَلْ تَشْعُرُ بِتَحَسُّنٍ اليَوْمَ؟

2M *hal taš3ur^u bi-taħassun^ini -lyawm^a?*

هَلْ تَشْعُرينَ بِتَحَسُّنٍ اليَوْمَ؟

2F *hal taš3urīn^a bi-taħassun^ini -lyawm^a?*

Are you feeling better today?

190

Track 4 - 6:03

عيدُ ميلادي في ديسَمْبِرَ.

3īd^u mīlādī fī dīsambir^a.

My birthday is in December.

191

Track 4 - 6:08

الكَلْبُ البُنِّيُّ الكَبيرُ وَدودٌ.

alkalb^{u} -lbunniyy^{u} -lkabīr^{u} wa-dūd^{un}.

The big brown dog is friendly.

192

Track 4 - 6:15

إِنَّها تَطْبُخُ العَشاءَ اللَّيْلَةَ.

ʔinnahā taṭbux^{u} -lʕašāʔ^{a} -llayla^{ta}.

She is cooking dinner tonight.

193

Track 4 - 6:21

إِنَّها تَأْكُلُ الغَداءَ في المَنْزِلِ.

ʔinnahā taʔkul^{u} -lɣadāʔ^{a} fī -lmanzil^{i}.

She is eating lunch at home.

194

Track 4 - 6:28

ما هِيَ أَهْدافُكَ؟

2M *mā hiya ʔahdāfuk^{a}?*

ما هِيَ أَهْدافُكِ؟

2F *mā hiya ʔahdāfuk^{i}?*

What are your goals?

195

Track 4 - 6:36

ماذا سَتَفْعَلُ اليَوْمَ؟

māđā sa-taf3al^u -lyawm^a?

What is she doing today?

196

Track 4 - 6:42

ماذا سَيَفْعَلُ اليَوْمَ؟

māđā sa-yaf3al^u -lyawm^a?

What is he doing today?

197

Track 4 - 6:47

سَوْفَ أَزورُ جَدَّيَّ.

sawf^a ʔazūr^u jaddayy^a.

I will visit my grandparents.

198

Track 4 - 6:52

أَنا مِنْ أُسْتُراليا.

ʔana min ʔusturālyā.

I'm from Australia.

199

Track 4 - 6:57

لَمْ أُشاهِدْ التِّلْفازَ.

lam ʔušāhid -ttilfāz^{a}.

I did not watch television.

200

Track 4 - 7:03

إِنَّها تُشاهِدُ التِّلْفازَ الْآنَ.

ʔinnahā tušāhid^{u} -ttilfāz^{a} -lʔān^{a}.

She is watching TV right now.

201

Track 5 - 0:00

هَلْ يُمْكِنُكَ أَنْ تُمَرِّرَ لِيَ المِلْحَ مِنْ فَضْلِكَ؟

2M *hal yumkinuk^{a} ʔan tumarrir^{a} liy^{a} -lmilħ^{a} min faḍlik^{a}?*

هَلْ يُمْكِنُكِ أَنْ تُمَرِّري لِيَ المِلْحَ مِنْ فَضْلِكِ؟

2F *hal yumkinuk^{i} ʔan tumarrirī liy^{a} -lmilħ^{a} min faḍlik^{i}?*

Can you please pass me the salt?

202

Track 5 - 0:17

الشَّجَرَةُ الخَضْراءُ الطَّويلَةُ جَميلَةٌ.

aššajara^{tu} -lxaḍrāʔ^{u} -ṭṭawīla^{tu} jamīla^{tun}.

The tall green tree is beautiful.

203

Track 5 - 0:24

لَمْ يُذاكِرْ لِلاخْتِبارِ وَرَسَبَ.

lam yuđākir li-lixtibār^{i} wa-rasab^{a}.

He didn't study for the test and failed.

204

Track 5 - 0:31

هَلْ يُمْكِنُني الحُصولُ عَلى كوبٍ
مِنَ الماءِ مِنْ فَضْلِكَ؟

2M *hal yumkinunī -lħuşūl^{u} 3alā kūb^{in}*
min^{a} -lmāʔ^{i} min faḑlik^{a}?

هَلْ يُمْكِنُني الحُصولُ عَلى كوبٍ
مِنَ الماءِ مِنْ فَضْلِكِ؟

2F *hal yumkinunī -lħuşūl^{u} 3alā kūb^{in}*
min^{a} -lmāʔ^{i} min faḑlik^{i}?

Can I have a glass of water, please?

205

Track 5 - 0:51

كانَ الطَّقْسُ لَطيفًا أَمْسِ.

kān^{a} -ţţaqs^{u} laţīfan ʔams^{i}.

The weather was nice yesterday.

206

Track 5 - 0:57

أَنْتَ لا تَذاكِرُ لِاخْتِبارِ الغَدِ.

2M *ʔant*^{a} *lā tađākir*^{u} *li-xtibār*^{i} *-lɣad*^{i}.

أَنْتِ لا تُذاكِرينَ لِاخْتِبارِ الغَدِ.

2F *ʔant*^{i} *lā tuđākirīn*^{a} *li-xtibār*^{i} *-lɣad*^{i}.

You are not studying for your test tomorrow.

207

Track 5 - 1:11

أَنْتَ تَمْشي إِلى المَتْجَرِ كُلَّ يَوْمٍ.

2M *ʔant*^{a} *tamšī ʔilā -lmatjar*^{i} *kull*^{a} *yawm*^{in}.

أَنْتِ تَمْشينَ إِلى المَتْجَرِ كُلَّ يَوْمٍ.

2F *ʔant*^{i} *tamšīn*^{a} *ʔilā -lmatjar*^{i} *kull*^{a} *yawm*^{in}.

You walk to the store every day.

208

Track 5 - 1:25

ما نَوْعُ الموسيقى المُفَضَّلُ لَدَيْكَ؟

2M *mā naw3*^{u} *-lmūsīqā -lmufaḍḍal*^{u} *ladayk*^{a}?

ما نَوْعُ الموسيقى المُفَضَّلُ لَدَيْكِ؟

2F *mā naw3*^{u} *-lmūsīqā -lmufaḍḍal*^{u} *ladayk*^{i}?

What is your favorite music genre?

209

Track 5 - 1:40

سَوْفَ أُقابِلُ صَديقي لِتَناوُلِ طَعامِ الغَداءِ.

3M *sawf^a ʔuqābil^u ṣadīqī li-tanāwul^i ṭa3ām^i -lɣadāʔ^i.*

سَوْفَ أُقابِلُ صَديقَتي لِتَناوُلِ طَعامِ الغَداءِ.

3F *sawf^a ʔuqābil^u ṣadīqatī li-tanāwul^i ṭa3ām^i -lɣadāʔ^i.*

I will meet my friend for lunch.

210

Track 5 - 1:59

هَلْ سَتَأْتي إِلى حَفْلَةِ عيدِ
ميلادي الأُسْبوعَ المُقْبِلَ؟

2M *hal sa-taʔtī ʔilā ɦafla^ti 3īd^i*
mīlādī -lʔusbū3^a -lmuqbil^a?

هَلْ سَتَأْتينَ إِلى حَفْلَةِ عيدِ
ميلادي الأُسْبوعَ المُقْبِلَ؟

2F *hal sa-taʔtīn^a ʔilā ɦafla^ti 3īd^i*
mīlādī -lʔusbū3^a -lmuqbil^a?

Will you come to my birthday party next week?

211

Track 5 - 2:20

لَدَيَّ القَليلُ مِنَ الواجِباتِ المَدْرَسِيَّةِ.

ladayy^a -lqalīl^u min^a -lwājibāt^i -lmadrasiyya^{ti}.

I have a little bit of homework.

212

Track 5 - 2:28

إِنَّها لا تُشاهِدُ التِّلْفازَ الآنَ.

ʔinnahā lā tušāhid^u -ttilfāz^a -lʔān^a.

She is not watching TV right now.

213

Track 5 - 2:35

أَنْتَ لَسْتَ عَلى ما يُرامُ اليَوْمَ.

2M *ʔant^a lasta 3alā mā yurām^u -lyawm^a.*

أَنْتِ لَسْتِ عَلى ما يُرامُ اليَوْمَ.

2F *ʔant^i last^i 3alā mā yurām^u -lyawm^a.*

You are not feeling well today.

214

Track 5 - 2:48

أَنْتَ ذَهَبْتَ إِلى المَتْحَفِ
في نِهايَةِ الأُسْبوعِ الماضي.

2M *ʔant^{a} đahabt^{a} ʔilā -lmatħaf^{i}*

fī nihāya^{ti} -lʔusbū3^{i} -lmāḍī.

أَنْتِ ذَهَبْتِ إِلى المَتْحَفِ
في نِهايَةِ الأُسْبوعِ الماضي.

2F *ʔant^{i} đahabt^{i} ʔilā -lmatħaf^{i}*

fī nihāya^{ti} -lʔusbū3^{i} -lmāḍī.

You went to the museum last weekend.

215

Track 5 - 3:08

جاءَ إِلى الِاجْتِماعِ.

jāʔ^{a} ʔilā -lijtimā3^{i}.

He came to the meeting.

216

Track 5 - 3:13

ماذا تَفْعَلُ في وَقْتِ فَراغِكَ؟

2M *māđā taf3al*^{u} *fī waqt*^{i} *farāɣik*^{a}*?*

ماذا تَفْعَلينَ في وَقْتِ فَراغِكِ؟

2F *māđā taf3alīn*^{a} *fī waqt*^{i} *farāɣik*^{i}*?*

What do you do in your free time?

217

Track 5 - 3:27

هَلْ سَتَأْتي إِلى مَنْزِلي لاحِقًا؟

2M *hal sa-taʔtī ʔilā manzilī lāħiqan?*

هَلْ سَتَأْتينَ إِلى مَنْزِلي لاحِقًا؟

2F *hal sa-taʔtīn*^{a} *ʔilā manzilī lāħiqan?*

Will you come over to my house later?

218

Track 5 - 3:40

هَلْ هِيَ تَمْشي إِلى العَمَلِ كُلَّ يَوْمٍ؟

hal hiya tamšī ʔilā -l3amal^{i} *kull*^{a} *yawm*^{in}*?*

Does she walk to work every day?

219

Track 5 - 3:48

أُحِبُّ لَعِبَ كُرَةِ القَدَمِ وَقِراءَةَ الكُتُبِ.

ʔuɦibb^{u} la3ib^{a} kura^{ti} -lqadam^{i} wa-qirāʔa^{ta} -lkutub^{i}.

I like to play soccer and read books.

220

Track 5 - 3:57

هَلْ تُذاكِرُ لِامْتِحاناتِكَ؟

2M *hal tuđākir^{u} li-mtiɦānātik^{a}?*

هَلْ تُذاكِرِينَ لِامْتِحاناتِكِ؟

2F *hal tuđākirīn^{a} li-mtiɦānātik^{i}?*

Are you studying for your exams?

221

Track 5 - 4:09

أَنْتَ لا تَنْتَبِهُ في الفَصْلِ.

2M *ʔant^{a} lā tantabih^{u} fī -lfaşl^{i}.*

أَنْتِ لا تَنْتَبِهِينَ في الفَصْلِ.

2F *ʔant^{i} lā tantabihīn^{i} fī -lfaşl^{i}.*

You are not paying attention in class.

222

Track 5 - 4:21

هَلْ تَسْتَطيعُ مُساعَدَتي في هَذا التَّمْرينِ؟

2M *hal tastaṭī3[u] musā3adatī fī hađā -ttamrīn[i]?*

هَلْ تَسْتَطيعينَ مُساعَدَتي في هَذا التَّمْرينِ؟

2F *hal tastaṭī3īn[a] musā3adatī fī hađā -ttamrīn[i]?*

Can you help me with this exercise?

223

Track 5 - 4:38

سَوْفَ يَذْهَبونَ إِلى الشّاطِئِ يَوْمَ السَّبْتِ.

sawf[a] yađhabūn[a] ʔilā -ššāṭiʔ[i] yawm[a] -ssabt[i].

They will go to the beach on Saturday.

224

Track 5 - 4:46

أَنْتَ لا تَأْكُلُ خُضْرَواتِكَ.

2M *ʔant[a] lā taʔkul[u] xuḍrawātik[a].*

أَنْتِ لا تَأْكُلينَ خُضْرَواتِكِ.

2F *ʔant[i] lā taʔkulīn[a] xuḍrawātik[i].*

You are not eating your vegetables.

225

Track 5 - 4:58

أَنا ذاهِبٌ لِزيارَةِ والِدي في نِهايَةِ هَذا الأُسْبوعِ.

1M *ʔana đāhib^un lizyāra^ti wālidī*

fī nihāya^ti hađā -lʔusbū3^i.

أَنا ذاهِبَةٌ لِزيارَةِ والِدي في نِهايَةِ هَذا الأُسْبوعِ.

1F *ʔana đāhiba^tun lizyāra^ti wālidī*

fī nihāya^ti hađā -lʔusbū3^i.

I'm going to visit my father this weekend.

226

Track 5 - 5:20

هِيَ لَنْ تَلْعَبَ كُرَةَ القَدَمِ اليَوْمَ.

hiya lan tal3ab^a kura^ta -lqadam^i -lyawm^a.

She is not going to play soccer today.

227

Track 5 - 5:26

هَلْ زُرْتَ أَيَّ دَوْلَةٍ أُخْرى؟

2M *hal zurt^a ʔayy^a dawla^tin ʔuxrā?*

هَلْ زُرْتِ أَيَّ دَوْلَةٍ أُخْرى؟

2F *hal zurt^i ʔayy^a dawla^tin ʔuxrā?*

Have you been to any other countries?

228

Track 5 - 5:38

هَلْ تَتَكَلَّمُ أَيَّ لُغَةٍ أُخْرى؟

2M *hal tatakallam^{u} ʔayy^{a} luɣa^{tin} ʔuxrā?*

هَلْ تَتَكَلَّمينَ أَيَّ لُغَةٍ أُخْرى؟

2F *hal tatakallamīn^{a} ʔayy^{a} luɣa^{tin} ʔuxrā?*

Do you speak any other languages?

229

Track 5 - 5:52

هَلْ تَرْتَدي حِذاءَكَ الجَديدَ اليَوْمَ؟

2M *hal tartadī ɧiđāʔak^{a} -ljadīd^{a} -lyawm^{a}?*

هَلْ تَرْتَدينَ حِذاءَكِ الجَديدَ اليَوْمَ؟

2F *hal tartadīn^{a} ɧiđāʔak^{i} -ljadīd^{a} -lyawm^{a}?*

Are you wearing your new shoes today?

230

Track 5 - 6:06

أَنا لَنْ أَذْهَبَ إِلى الشّاطِئِ اليَوْمَ.

ʔana lan ʔađhab^{a} ʔilā -ššāṭiʔ^{i} -lyawm^{a}.

I'm not going to the beach today.

231

Track 5 - 6:13

لَنْ نَلْتَقي بِصَديقِنا لِتَناوُلِ طَعامِ الغَداءِ.

3M *lan naltaqī bi-ṣadīqinā li-tanāwul^{i} ṭa3ām^{i} -lɣadāʔ^{i}.*

لَنْ نَلْتَقي بِصَديقَتِنا لِتَناوُلِ طَعامِ الغَداءِ.

3F *lan naltaqī bi-ṣadīqatinā li-tanāwul^{i} ṭa3ām^{i} -lɣadāʔ^{i}.*

We will not meet our friend for lunch.

232

Track 5 - 6:33

لَقَدْ شاهَدَتْ الفيلْمَ وَأَحَبَّتْهُ.

laqad šāhadat -lfīlm^{a} wa-ʔaħabbath^{u}.

She saw the movie and loved it.

233

Track 5 - 6:40

لَقَدْ شاهَدَ الفيلْمَ وَلَكِنَّهُ لَمْ يُعْجِبْهُ.

laqad šāhad^{a} -lfīlm^{a} wa-lakinnah^{u} lam yu3jibh^{u}.

He saw the movie, but he didn't like it.

234

Track 5 - 6:48

كانَ لَوْني المُفَضَّلُ هُوَ الأَسْوَدُ.

kān^{a} lawnī -lmufaḍḍal^{u} huwa -lʔaswad^{u}.

My favorite color used to be black.

235

Track 5 - 6:55

لَمْ أَزُرْ جَدَّيَّ أَمْسِ.

lam ʔazur jaddayy^a ʔams^i.

I did not visit my grandparents yesterday.

236

Track 5 - 7:01

هَلْ يُمْكِنُكَ التَّحَدُّثُ بِبُطْءٍ أَكْثَرَ مِنْ فَضْلِكَ؟

2M *hal yumkinuk^a -ttaɦaddut^u*

bi-buṭʔ^in ʔaktar^a min faḍlik^a?

هَلْ يُمْكِنُكِ التَّحَدُّثُ بِبُطْءٍ أَكْثَرَ مِنْ فَضْلِكِ؟

2F *hal yumkinuk^i -ttaɦaddut^u*

bi-buṭʔ^in ʔaktar^a min faḍlik^i?

Can you speak more slowly, please?

237

Track 5 - 7:19

لَمْ أَذْهَبْ إِلى الشّاطِئِ أَمْسِ.

lam ʔađhab ʔilā -ššāṭiʔ^i ʔams^i.

I did not go to the beach yesterday.

238

Track 5 - 7:25

كَيْفَ تَقولُ ______ بِاللُّغَةِ العَرَبِيَّةِ؟

2M *kayf[a] taqūl[u] ______ bi-lluɣa[ti] -l3arabiyya[ti]?*

كَيْفَ تَقولينَ ______ بِاللُّغَةِ العَرَبِيَّةِ؟

2F *kayf[a] taqūlīn[a] ______ bi-lluɣa[ti] -l3arabiyya[ti]?*

How do you say ______ in Arabic?

239

Track 5 - 7:41

ماذا تُحِبُّ أَنْ تَفْعَلَ في وَقْتِ فَراغِكَ؟

2M *māđā tuɦibb[u] ʔan taf3al[a] fī waqt[i] farāɣik[a]?*

ماذا تُحِبّينَ أَنْ تَفْعَلي في وَقْتِ فَراغِكِ؟

2F *māđā tuɦibbīn[a] ʔan taf3alī fī waqt[i] farāɣik[i]?*

What do you like to do in your free time?

240

Track 5 - 7:59

ماذا تَدْرُسُ في المَدْرَسَةِ؟

2M *māđā tadrus[u] fī -lmadrasa[ti]?*

ماذا تَدْرُسينَ في المَدْرَسَةِ؟

2F *māđā tadrusīn[a] fī -lmadrasa[ti]?*

What are you studying in school?

241

Track 5 - 8:11

هِيَ لا تَأْكُلُ في مَطْعَمٍ.

hiya lā taʔkul^{u} *fī maṭ3am*^{in}*.*

She is not eating at a restaurant.

242

Track 5 - 8:16

ما هِيَ أَهْدافُكَ المُسْتَقْبَلِيَّةُ؟

2M *mā hiya ʔahdāfuk*^{a} *-lmustaqbaliyya*^{tu}*?*

ما هِيَ أَهْدافُكِ المُسْتَقْبَلِيَّةُ؟

2F *mā hiya ʔhdāfuk*^{i} *-lmustaqbaliyya*^{tu}*?*

What are your goals for the future?

243

Track 5 - 8:29

عيدُ ميلادِ والِدي الشَّهْرُ المُقْبِلُ.

3īd^{u} *mīlād*^{i} *wālidī -ššahr*^{u} *-lmuqbil*^{u}*.*

My father's birthday is next month.

244

Track 5 - 8:37

أَنْتَ لَمْ تُنْهِ واجِبَكَ المَدْرَسيَّ اللَّيْلَةَ الماضِيَّةَ.

2M *ʔant^{a} lam tunhi wājibak^{a} -lmadrasyy^{a}*
-llayla^{ta} -lmāḍiyya^{ta}.

أَنْتِ لَمْ تُنْهي واجِبَكِ المَدْرَسيَّ
اللَّيْلَةَ الماضيَةَ.

2F *ʔant^{i} lam tunhī wājibak^{i} -lmadrasyy^{a}*
-llayla^{ta} -lmāḍya^{ta}.

You did not finish your homework last night.

245

Track 5 - 8:56

يَعْمَلُ والِدي كَطَبيبٍ في مُسْتَشْفًى.

ya3mal^{u} wālidī kaṭabīb^{in} fī mustašfā^{n}.

My father works as a doctor at a hospital.

246

Track 5 - 9:04

سَوْفَ يَزورونَ جَدَّيْهِمْ غَدًا.

sawf^{a} yazūrūn^{a} jaddayhim ɣadan.

They will visit their grandparents tomorrow.

247

Track 5 - 9:11

أنا أَعْمَلُ في مَدْرَسَةٍ كَمُدَرِّسٍ.

1M *ʔana ʔa3mal^{u} fī madrasa^{tin} kamudarris^{in}.*

أنا أَعْمَلُ في مَدْرَسَةٍ كَمُدَرِّسَةٍ.

1F *ʔana ʔa3mal^{u} fī madrasa^{tin} kamudarrisa^{tin}.*

I work at a school as a teacher.

248

Track 5 - 9:26

سَوْفَ تَذْهَبُ لِلْعَمَلِ غَدًا.

2M *sawf^{a} tađhab^{u} li-l3amal^{i} ɣadan.*

سَوْفَ تَذْهَبينَ لِلْعَمَلِ غَدًا.

2F *sawf^{a} tađhabīn^{a} li-l3amal^{i} ɣadan.*

You will go to work tomorrow.

249

Track 5 - 9:39

أَنا آسِفٌ، لَيْسَ لَدَيَّ ما يَكْفي مِنَ المالِ.

1M *ʔana ʔāsif^{un}, lays^{a} ladayy^{a} mā yakfī min^{a} -lmāl^{i}.*

أَنا آسِفَةٌ، لَيْسَ لَدَيَّ ما يَكْفي مِنَ المالِ.

1F *ʔana ʔāsifa^{tun}, lays^{a} ladayy^{a} mā yakfī min^{a} -lmāl^{i}.*

I'm sorry, I don't have enough money.

250

Track 5 - 9:58

كَيْفَ يَبْدو جَدْوَلُ عَمَلِكَ؟

2M *kayf*^{a} *yabdū jadwal*^{u} *3amalik*^{a}*?*

كَيْفَ يَبْدو جَدْوَلُ عَمَلِكِ؟

2F *kayf*^{a} *yabdū jadwal*^{u} *3amalik*^{i}*?*

What is your work schedule like?

Printed in Great Britain
by Amazon

40470902R00046